Social media for Decorators

The evergreen guide to using social media as a Painter & Decorator

By

Jon Mears

www.jmears.co.uk

INTRODUCTION

There's no shortage of people claiming to have the latest tips and tricks when it comes to social media.

In fact, if you Google 'Social media tips' you'll get over 5 billion results.

People will tell you to use certain hashtags, post at certain times of day, turn still images in 5 second videos and all sorts of other rubbish.

Don't get me wrong, most of these tips can give you marginal improvements, but these techniques are all based on trying to 'beat the algorithm' and rarely work for very long.

These 'tips' fail to teach you the evergreen truths to getting the most out of social media.

This book is not going to teach you any hacks or tricks.

This book is going to give you the understanding you need to be successful on any social media platform both now and in the future.

For me, there are just two things you need to understand to be successful with social media.

1. How social media platforms make money
2. Basic human behaviour

But before we dive into these two points, I have already mentioned the great and mysterious 'algorithm', and I need to cover off what it actually is.

When you log on to any social media platform, the order in which the posts are shown to you are decided by an algorithm.

An algorithm is a piece of code that tries to learn as much about you as possible, so that it can show you the posts you are most likely to enjoy.

Example:

Let's say your partner posts photographs of your children on Facebook regularly.

Every time you see these photos on your Facebook feed, you take time to look at them, you 'like' them and you comment on them.

Now let's say your auntie tends to post videos of her cats on Facebook.

You're not really interested in this. So, you don't tend to watch more than a few seconds of the videos and you never comment on the posts.

The job of the algorithm is to learn what posts you like to see, and make sure they are at the top of your feed whenever you open the app.

In this case, that means that every time your partner posts a photo of the children, this shoots to the top of your feed and is the first thing you see.

But you don't see your auntie's videos until you've scrolled through all the other stuff the algorithm thinks you'll like more.

This is why you tend to see the same 5-10 people on your Facebook feed every day, and you hardly ever see posts from the hundreds of other friends you have.

Why does the algorithm do this?

This gets me on to the first thing you need to understand to be successful on social media. How they make money.

The reason social media is free to use is because advertisers pay to have their ads pop up on your feed as you scroll.

In order to show you more ads (and therefore make more money) social media platforms need to keep you engaged.

They want you to come back to the platform more regularly and keep scrolling for longer.

The algorithm is the key to this.

By learning everything it can about you and then tailoring the content you see, you'll spend more time on the platform.

Literally every social media feed is personalized to the user by an algorithm.

Try it if you don't believe me.

Scroll through your partners Facebook or Instagram for 5 minutes. It'll seem totally different to yours, even though you probably share a lot of the same friends.

Have you ever heard the following quote?

'If you are not paying for it, you're not the customer; you're the product being sold'

This sums up social media for me.

Now that we understand how social media platforms make their money, you need to get to grips with the second point.

Basic human behaviour.

Don't worry, this isn't half as complicated as it might seem.

All you need to know is that no matter how many hashtags, hacks, tips and tricks you use, if the content you post doesn't **inform**, **entertain** or **connect** your audience then you won't get very far.

If you post boring stuff all day long, then the algorithm will relegate you to the bottom of people's feed.

If you want people to see your posts and engage with you then you need to teach them things, you need to make them laugh or cry, you need to connect them to people.

Understand these two golden principles and you're well on the way to social media success.

TABLE OF CONTENTS

Legal Notes

First published in the United Kingdom in 2022

First edition September 2022

CHAPTER 1 – WHY DO YOU NEED A SOCIAL MEDIA STRATEGY?

A few weeks ago, a decorator reached out to me to ask for some advice on some Facebook ads he was running.

The ads seemed to be performing well. He'd received 10 new enquiries in the first few days.

The problem was that after pricing up these 10 jobs, nobody had responded to his quotes yet.

Usually when he sent a quote out, the customer would respond within a day or two. Sometimes even the same afternoon!

However, several days after quoting for the Facebook ad enquiries he'd heard nothing.

So, why was this happening? And how did we fix it?

The reason this was happening was because the enquiries were coming from people at a different stage of the 'buyer journey'

Let me quickly explain the buyer journey from a marketing perspective.

Before any purchasing decision is made, a buyer goes through 4 stages:

Stage 1: Unaware of the problem. On average 60% of your potential market are unaware they have a problem that needs solving.

Stage 2: Aware of the problem, but not actively looking for solutions. This section of people accounts for around 20% of your market.

Stage 3: Consideration. This section of the market is aware of the problem and are actively considering different solutions to the problem. These people make up around 17% of your market.

Stage 4: Decision. The final 3% of the market are the people who know what they want to do and are actively making decisions on getting some decorating work done.

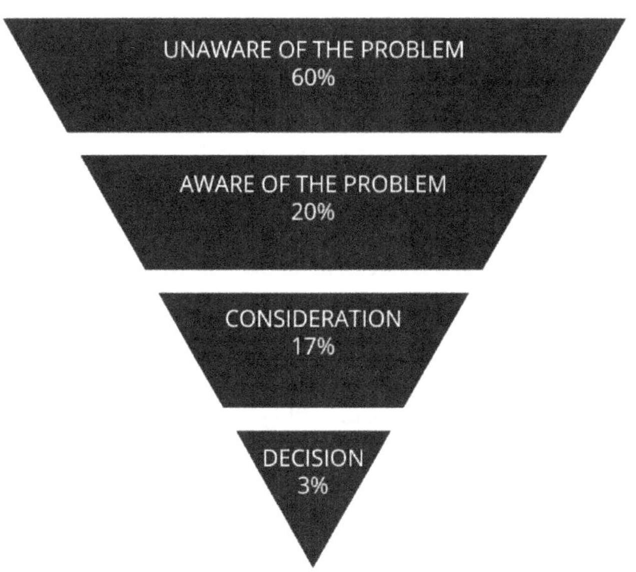

Before running Facebook ads, this decorator got all his work from word of mouth.

Now, when you put 'word of mouth' customers into the buyer journey, you'll realise they are already at stage 4.

They already knew they had a problem and had decided they needed decorating work to solve it.

They asked friends for recommendations and considered them.

They then reached out to the decorator as they were ready to make the decision.

At which point, as long as the quote came in at around the price they were expecting, they'd accept it straight away.

Now think about where the buyer is on the journey when they click on a Facebook ad.

They are more likely to be in stage 3 'consideration'. They could potentially still be in stage 2.

For the decorator who contacted me, this meant he wasn't getting quick responses to his quotes.

Afterall, if the potential customer is still in the 'consideration' stage they will be getting quotes from other decorators, they'll be talking to friends to see if they have any recommendations, they might even be considering a different type of work all together. Decorating might not be the only solution to their problem.

So, what happened?

Well, over time, some of the quotes came back and were accepted but it wasn't as many as he would have expected.

This leads me to the question in the title of this chapter.

'Why do you need a social media strategy?'

Social media is a fantastic way to expand on your other marketing efforts, to grow your brand awareness and turn potential customers into buyers.

Let me point out a key phrase in that last sentence: *'Expand on your* ***other*** *marketing efforts'*

Social media should complement what you are already doing. It shouldn't be the *only* thing you are doing.

Now, if you're going to use social media to develop your decorating business, then you need understand the buyer journey and build a plan to take potential customers through it.

The decorator I spoke with jumped in blind with his Facebook ads and was unprepared for what happened.

It wasn't a disaster by any means. Afterall, he got some work from it. And he has also learned how he can improve next time.

This is basically how I learned about the buyer journey. By jumping in blind, making mistakes, and learning from them.

The good news for you, is that now I can share a better way to do it, so you can get a superior return on your marketing spend.

The plan:

As we discovered, your potential market can be broken down into the 4 stages of the buyer's journey.

The job of your social media strategy is to guide them through each stage.

To do this, you need to develop tactics for each stage of the journey.

Stage 1: Unaware of the problem

To move someone from stage 1 to stage 2 you need make them aware of the problem. An example of this would be to write an article or post a video educating people on how to identify when you need to re-paint your exterior.

You could write an article about all the warning signs that the paint is failing. Rot, mould, chalkiness, flaking, cracks, faded colour etc.

You could take photos or videos of jobs you are working on that are suffering with these issues.

You could even get a testimonial from a customer where they explain the problem they were having and how you solved it for them.

If it's not exterior work, then think about the other jobs you do. Kitchen cabinet painting is growing in popularity and lots of people are still completely unaware that it is even possible. So, educate people on the processes you use and the benefits of re-painting rather than replacing.

Stage 2: Aware of the problem

To get someone from stage 2 to stage 3 you need to show people why they need to start looking for solutions. You need to inject some urgency into the matter.

As an example, let's say you specialise in painting kitchens. You could talk about how painting your kitchen will make you proud to host your family for Christmas. Or how it can make your home much easier to sell.

Think about how often you're on a job where you're stain blocking watermarks or mould on a bathroom ceiling. If you take photos or film this process, you'll show people how easily you can solve this problem for them. Pair this up with a caption that explains how the customer had visitors coming over soon and didn't want the embarrassment of a mouldy bathroom and you've injected the urgency that moves them on to stage 3!

Stage 3: Consideration

The next step is moving them from stage 3 to 4. At this point your potential customer is considering all potential options. So, your job is to use things like case studies, videos and social media to educate and inspire them.

Think about what they might be searching online. It'll likely be things like 'how to save money painting and decorating' or 'interior design ideas for living rooms'

You could attract people like this with articles about the latest colour trends in the industry or 'before and after' transformation photos of recent jobs. You could even write a blog listing out a few things customers can do to save money on hiring painters and decorators. Educate them that buying the paint themselves won't save them money!

And don't forget that there are other solutions to a lot of the problems you solve. For example, the customer might be looking at replacing their windows rather than having them repainted.

Use social media to explain the cost saving benefits to repainting rather than replacing. Show them the difference in finish a professional will get on kitchen cabinets compared to a DIY job.

Stage 4: Decision

Up until now, all you've done is provide useful information to potential buyers. This has done wonders for your brand awareness and how people feel about your company.

As the person who has guided them through the buyer journey you are now top of the list to be hired. And you've done all of it without actually asking them to buy from you. Great isn't it!

What you've done already should give you a steady flow of new customers.

However, if you want to give them a final little nudge, or top up the number of enquiries you're getting this is where you can post some ads saying things like 'Taking bookings for Summer now' or 'space has just opened up for next month – get in touch to discuss your needs'

Now you know why you need a social media strategy, it's time to build it!

CHAPTER 2 – THE 4 PILLARS OF YOUR SOCIAL MEDIA STRATEGY

PILLAR 1 – DEFINING YOUR IDEAL CUSTOMER PERSONA (ICP)

Before you can start effectively communicating on social media, you need to know who you are, and who you are talking to.

The first part is easy when you are the owner of a small decorating firm, or you're a sole trader. You know who you are and how you want to present yourself on social media.

The second part is a bit more complicated.

Who are you talking to?

One of the most common mistakes businesses make when using social media is they try to talk to everyone at once. They try and attract all types of customers and their posts look more like generic broadcasts than conversations.

Here's an example of a couple of social media captions:

1. 'Here at HGA Decorators we pride ourselves on attention to detail in our work.'
2. 'Try using darker colours on ceilings and painting down to the picture rail. It'll make any snug or cinema room feel much cosier. Here's some photos of one we completed recently in Oxford. Colour is Farrow & Ball Railings.'

The first caption is very generic and uninspiring. The second caption is the complete opposite.

The second caption inspires and educates the customer on design ideas. It also speaks to a much narrower audience, as it mentions 'Oxford' and 'snug or cinema room'.

Now, if you're a decorator based in Oxford who likes to work in expensive homes, which of the two captions is more likely attract your target customer?

The answer is simple isn't it.

So, before I explain how to define your Ideal Customer Persona (ICP) let me debunk the most common pushback I get about this.

Q: *'Aren't I better off trying to appeal to a larger audience? Won't I attract fewer customers if I get too specific on who I want to work for? Won't I lose out on potential jobs?'*

A: No. You'll actually get more work the more specific you are.

Think about this book. It's called 'Social media for **decorators'**. Would you be reading it if I'd written 'Social media for the trades' or even 'Social media for small businesses'. Probably not. You definitely wouldn't have bought it if it was called 'Social media for business'

There are literally thousands of books about social media, and yet I'd bet that this is one of the few you've actually bought. It might even be the only one.

If I'd have written the book 'Social media for business' I'd probably sell 0 copies. It's simply too generic.

Yes, it technically appeals to a larger audience. But it doesn't appeal to anyone quite enough to make them actually buy it.

For someone to buy something, it helps if it appeals specifically to them.

In my case, that means writing specifically for decorators.

In your case, that means talking to people who specifically match the service you offer, where you offer it and for the price you offer it for!

So, let's build your Ideal Customer Persona (ICP), so you know who you are specifically trying to attract.

I find the best thing to do when building your ICP is to base it on a customer you've dealt with in the past. This makes it more real.

Here's an example of what your ICP *could* look like if you're a residential decorator based in Oxford:

Name: Harriet

Age: 72

Location: Oxford

Occupation: Retired doctor

Status: Married, 3 grown up children, 2 grand children

Interests: Health and fitness, medical research, the environment, hosting dinner parties, looking after grand children

This might seem like very basic information, but it gives us a real insight into Harriet. And knowing this will help you with 3 very important things.

1. **Your tone of voice** – Now you can see Harriet and you know the sort of person she is; you know how to talk to her. If I'm writing a caption

on social media and Harriet is my ICP, then I'm not going to be swearing or referencing memes. This isn't how I'd speak to someone like Harriet in real life, so it's not what I'm going to do on social media. My 'tone of voice' is going to be professional, respectful, and informative, as I think this is what Harriet would respond best to.

If my ICP was a 20-year-old guy called Alex, then I might be more inclined to use memes and drop in the odd swear word as that's how I'd speak to him in real life.

2. **The content she wants from you** – What would Harriet want you to talk about on social media? Well, based on her interests you could talk about the environmental benefits of painting kitchen cabinets instead of replacing them. You could inspire her with before and after pictures of beautiful dining rooms. You could explain how you always use durable paints that are scrubbable. Perfect for when she has the grandchildren over!
3. **Where to find her** – Is Harriet on Tik Tok? Unlikely. Is she on Instagram? Maybe. LinkedIn? Probably. Facebook? Almost certainly. Now you know this you can stop wasting your time creating Tik Toks all day. Instead, you can focus on being active on Facebook and LinkedIn. As this is where Harriet is most likely to see you!

Now, your ICP might look nothing like Harriet. Yours might be more like Alex. And this might mean you focus on Tik Tok and Instagram. And it might mean you post memes and fun content. It doesn't matter who your ICP is. All that matters is that you know who they are and build your social media strategy accordingly.

Task: Create your ICP and write down the details for them. Find a stock image like I did too. Visualising your ICP like this will help with a lot of your marketing work going forward.

Throughout this book I'll be regularly referring to Harriet and your ICP, and you'll see just how important it is to have one!

PILLAR 2 – SETTING THE RIGHT GOALS

Setting goals and targets sounds like the sort of thing only big corporate businesses do. But having the right goals and knowing how to measure them is crucial to any business.

Setting goals gives your business direction.

If you set the wrong goal, or don't set a goal at all, then you might end up going in the wrong direction. This could ultimately lead to the downfall of your business.

So, how do you set the right social media goals for your business?

The first thing people tend to do when they think about social media goals is increasing their followers or the amount of likes they get on posts.

Here's the thing. Likes and follows won't pay the bills.

They are vanity metrics, and you need to stop worrying about them so much.

Don't get me wrong, having lots of followers and likes is not a bad thing. In fact, it's a great indicator that what you're doing is working. However, this shouldn't be the basis of all your goals.

Think about what you actually want to get out of social media.

Let's say your goal is to get more enquiries.

How can you do this?

The place to start is with something called S.M.A.R.T goals.

Yes, I know…it's a corporate acronym. I usually despise these as much as the next person, but this one is actually decent. I promise!

S.M.A.R.T stands for Specific. Measurable. Achievable. Relevant. Time.

Let's run the goal of getting more enquiries through S.M.A.R.T.

Specific: 'Get more enquiries' is a bit too vague. Think about how we can make it more specific so we can focus our efforts.

Remember our ICP from earlier? We know that Harriet is most often found on Facebook. So why don't we update our goal accordingly.

'Get more enquiries' becomes 'Get more enquiries from Facebook'

Measurable: This sounds simple right? You simply measure the number of enquiries you get.

The problem with this is you can't fully control the number of people who enquire.

What you can do though, is measure things that you know tend to lead to enquiries.

For example, you could say with reasonable certainty that the more often you post content on Facebook, the more enquiries you tend to get.

So, your measurable goal could be to post on Facebook 3 times a week.

You see how we have changed the goal from something you can't control (get more enquiries) to something you can control (post 3 times a week).

Now you have control, let's move on to the next step.

Achievable: Is posting 3 times a week achievable? What does this involve you doing? This might mean you set aside 15 minutes a day to create content. You could use these 15 minutes to edit photos, to create a video or simply just to think of new ideas.

Relevant: Is your goal relevant to your business as a whole? Do you actually want more enquiries from Facebook? Or are you better off focusing on something else?

Time: The final component is to set a time frame. If you don't, you'll end up putting it off.

When are you going to start doing this? And how long are you going to do it for?

Work this out and let's look at your final goal.

Remember, we started with the goal 'get more enquiries'

Now we have the goal, 'Spend 15 minutes a day creating content for Facebook, so I can post 3 times per week for the next 6 months'

See the difference?

We've gone from a very generic goal, to something that gives us a real focus.

Now all that would be left to do is measure how many enquiries you got in the previous 6 months and compare it to how many you got after 6 months with your new goal.

Then you simply review the results and tweak your S.M.A.R.T goal accordingly.

PILLAR 3 – LISTENING AND LEARNING

People often forget that social media is not just about posting content all the time.

You can learn a lot of valuable information just by sitting back and listening to the conversations that are already going on.

Think about your ICP and what you can learn about them using social media.

Let's take Harriet as our example again.

We know where Harriet lives and her general interests, plus, we know she is generally found on Facebook.

I would make an educated guess that she is often found in Facebook communities (formerly Facebook groups).

Now we know this, we can spend time in these communities too.

Once inside, we can 'listen' to the conversations that Harriet (and customers like her) are having. We can see the problems they face and the solutions they recommend to each other.

Look for the problems you can solve.

If you can become an active and valuable member of the communities Harriet is in this will do wonders for your brand and your business as a whole.

Pillar 4 – Creating Content That Serves

Why do you think most businesses don't get the results they want from social media?

The most common reason I see for this is to do with mindset.

When it comes to using social media as a business, people tend to adopt the mindset of:

'What can my business get out of this?'

Weirdly, most people with unsuccessful business social media accounts, have very popular personal accounts.

This is because when they post on their personal account, they have the mindset of:

'What are my friends getting out of this?'

On their personal account all their posts are designed to make their friends laugh or help them.

Whereas on their business account they are constantly trying to get something out of their audience. 'Call now for a quote' or 'Taking bookings for exterior decorating now'

Ironically, all the people on their personal social media feed wouldn't hesitate to recommend them. However, most of the people seeing their business social media would struggle to remember the company name.

As you can see, the solution is clear.

You must change your focus from yourself, to your potential customers.

Your social media should be serving them, not you.

Be entertaining and informative. Show your human side. In the same way you do on your personal social media!

Stop just broadcasting messages about your business and start having conversations with your audience instead. Find ways to give them value. Be social!

Making this change isn't as easy as it might seem but stick with it and play the long game. It will pay off.

For a great example of a business with great social media. Check out Innocent smoothies.

All their content is fun and feels like it could have been written by your best friend.

But they still manage to keep everything on the theme of their business.

CHAPTER 4 – WHICH SOCIAL MEDIA CHANNELS SHOULD I USE?

One of the most common questions I get asked by decorators is: Which social media channels should I use?

The answer is simple. It's whatever social media platform your ICP uses. And remember, this might change over time.

Harriet currently tends to use Facebook and LinkedIn. But one day she might switch to Instagram.

In 10 years time Instagram might not exist. Harriet might be using a new social media platform that hasn't been invented yet.

The trick is to use the 80/20 rule.

Spend 80% of your time focused on the platform your ICP uses and spend 20% of your time keeping a basic presence on the other channels.

This is important because you don't want to have all your eggs in one basket.

You never know what's going to happen tomorrow.

Now, I'm writing this book to be 'evergreen', but I think it'll still be useful to do a quick run through of the top social media channels as they stand in 2022 as it may help you to better identify where you're likely to find your ICP, and how to communicate with them on each platform.

Facebook

The king of social media. At time of writing, nearly 3 billion people are on Facebook. With almost 2 billion of them being daily users.

If you're looking for your ICP, there is a strong chance you'll find them on Facebook! Especially if they are slightly older. The amount of Facebook users over 60 years old is increasing year on year.

Here's something you might not know.

I don't really like Facebook.

I find it can often be quite a toxic place.

However, used correctly it can be amazing.

The reason I use Facebook, even though I think it can be toxic, is because my personal ICP is found there.

Fortunately, my ICP is also found in the corners of Facebook that isn't so toxic! This is how I manage to make it work for me.

Facebook's mission is: *To give people the power to build community and bring the world closer together.*

And to be fair, I think they do a very good job of this.

Facebook does feel very personal. It is a great place to connect with friends, family and communities with similar interests.

Bear this in mind when you are using Facebook to connect with your ICP.

People want to see your human side on Facebook. They want to feel connected with you.

It is not a place to blast out advertisements for your business. It's a place to connect with your community.

Use Facebook communities (formerly Facebook groups) to learn about your ICP and connect with them.

INSTAGRAM

My personal favourite...Instagram.

Instagram started as quite an arty place. People would use it to show off their photography skills and not much else.

However, more and more people are migrating to Instagram as it's a fun and dare I say, less toxic place to be compared to Facebook.

The average age of an Instagram user tends to be slightly younger than that of Facebook, but you'll find a good mix of people.

Overall, I think the platform has developed into a great way to connect with your ICP and it is a brilliant place for you as a decorator to show photos of your work and inspire potential customers.

TWITTER

Twitter can be a tricky place to connect with your ICP, but it is possible.

Lots of conversations happen on Twitter and it's easy for you to jump in and help where you can.

Twitter has traditionally been the place to get up to the minute news.

Things move quickly on here, so you need to do the same.

Use Twitter as a place to learn about what questions your ICP has. Answer them if you can, and don't be afraid to showcase your work here.

YOUTUBE

Often referred to as the world's second biggest search engine, YouTube is chronically underused by decorators.

Earlier in the book we talked about the buyer journey.

Part of that journey is the 'consideration' stage.

During this stage, your ICP wants to learn about all possible solutions to their problem. They do this by asking questions. And where do they ask these questions? Google and YouTube.

As a social media platform, YouTube is the perfect place to guide your ICP through this stage of the buyer journey.

You don't need to have hundreds of videos up and you don't need to post weekly blogs. But if you can create videos that answer common questions your ICP has, then you'll find huge success here.

LinkedIn

Advertised as the 'Professional network', LinkedIn offers exactly what you'd expect.

It's a place to connect with the more professional ICP.

If you are looking for commercial clients, LinkedIn is a great place to be.

Remember that LinkedIn is a more formal platform that most, and it is less personal.

If your ICP is on LinkedIn, then I suggest you focus on educating them with your posts.

Show the sort of work you do and show them the processes involved to achieve those results.

LinkedIn is less a place people go to get design inspiration and more a place to learn about what is involved in getting a good decorating job.

TIK TOK, SNAPCHAT, REDDIT AND ALL THE OTHERS…

Social media platforms will always come and go. Some will be more popular than others. Platforms like TikTok and Snapchat can be very effective for your business, and you shouldn't discard them.

A lot of people didn't bother when TikTok came out as they thought it was just for silly dances.

But some decorators tried it, and it changed the entire course of their business!

My advice is to always be on the lookout for the next big thing.

As I said earlier, focus 80% of your time on your main channel, but keep 20% of your time for everything else. You never know what's going to happen.

CHAPTER 5 – CREATING GREAT CONTENT

Probably the toughest thing about using social media for your business is knowing what to post.

Once again, we need to refer back to Harriet.

Think about things from the perspective of your ICP. What do they want to see? How can you serve them? How can you be informative, entertaining or even inspirational?

A common mistake for decorators is using social media to try and impress other decorators.

Showing off prep skills or what settings they have their heated hose at.

If you're doing this because you are trying to educate and elevate the painting and decorating industry, then thank you. However, if you're doing this and expecting Harriet to be impressed, you're going to be disappointed.

Think about what your ICP is interested in and what they might like to see.

In the case of Harriet, we know she is the sort of person who enjoys having guests over for dinner. With this in mind, we can create some content that will inspire her.

Posting an image of a freshly painted kitchen or dining room would be very useful for Harriet to see. Tell her what colours you used, what wallpaper design it is and how long it took. But don't bother telling her what type of filler you used and what your favourite sash brush is. Harriet couldn't care less about that sort of thing!

Consider this, decorators often talk about how amazing Farrow & Ball or Little Greene marketing is. Some will even moan about it! And yet, very few decorators model their own marketing on it.

Notice I'm not saying copy. I'm saying model.

Go through the Farrow & Ball social media pages and website one day. It is all focused on inspiring their ICP with colour and design ideas. And guess what? Their ICP is probably just like yours!

These huge paint companies spend millions on marketing strategies to attract customers just like yours. Why don't you try and learn from what they are doing and implement it to your strategy?

Let's look at the different types of content you can use on social media and how to get the most out of them.

PHOTOS

Luckily for you, social media is a very visual place. And you do work that is very visual. So, photos will be the bread and butter of your content plan.

One of the most powerful things in marketing is the classic 'before and after' photo.

Everyone loves a transformation. Whether it's a fat person who is now slim, or a tired old bedroom that has been decorated into something beautiful.

But remember, your ICP is scrolling through hundreds of images and videos on social media. So, your photo needs to stand out or Harriet won't stop scrolling!

For this reason, I think we need to rename the 'before and after' post, to the 'after and before' post.

I'll refer to Farrow and Ball again. Have a look at their Instagram page and see how many of their posts start with a 'before' image.

Actually, I'll save you the time. It's none of them.

They know that to get people to stop scrolling you need to show them something beautiful. So, the first image on your post should be the 'after' image. It should be the one that makes Harriet say 'oh, I love that colour. I should do my dining room like that'

The second thing you need to know when it comes to posting photos on social media is that quality counts.

Too many decorators spend days and weeks painstakingly creating a beautiful room, showing the most incredible attention to detail and then…take a rubbish photo and go home.

I've spoken about it before and I'm sure I'll speak about it again hundreds of times. You need to take more care with your photography. Don't short change yourself with poor photos. Your work deserves better.

Here are my top tips for getting better photos for your social media (and no, you don't need a fancy camera. Just use your phone)

1. Shoot into the corner of a room to make the space look bigger and to use the natural lines of the room to lead the eye into the centre of the shot.
2. Height is important. Take your shots from about mid-height. Try to capture equal amounts of ceiling and floor in the frame. Make sure all your images are from this height. Consistency is key. For most people the correct height will be around their belly button. So just remember that!
3. Tidy up! There is nothing worse than seeing charging cables hanging out or tools in the background. Imagine you're trying to get the perfect image to go on the front cover of a magazine.
4. If possible, only use natural light. Turn off all other light sources. This will give you better colours and highlights.
5. Experiment with angles. Take a few shots from each corner of the room and see what looks best.
6. Don't abuse the 'wide angle'. These types of shots can look great, but they often distort the

image and make the whole room look very odd.

7. Keep your lines straight. Use uprights and doors to ensure all lines in your image are straight. If you go to the camera settings on your phone you can turn on a grid. I'd recommend doing this as it helps you line everything up.
8. Photograph the room, not just your work. It's tempting just to capture an image of your work, but photos need context. A picture of a feature wall taken from straight on very rarely makes a good photo. You need to imagine you are showing off the whole room. It'll make the photo more interesting and more appealing to the eye. Think about it from Harriet's point of view. She wants help visualising how her room might look if she hires you. She doesn't want a close up shot of the 2 pack filling you did.
9. Mix it up with close detail shots. Don't be afraid to get a little artsy! Experiment with close ups on certain features.
10. Zoom with your feet. If you want to zoom in on a shot, try to avoid using the zoom function on the phone. It's just not as good as actually walking forwards a few steps.
11. Edit all your photos! Before you post a photo, just take a couple of minutes to tweak the basics. Brightness, contrast, saturation etc. There are loads of free apps you can do this

on, and it makes a big difference. So, make sure you do it.

12. Clean your lens! Please give the back of your phone a wipe before taking photos. Not doing that can ruin all the hard work above!

VIDEO

The very fact that there are social media platforms dedicated to video (YouTube & TikTok) proves that video needs to be part of your social media strategy.

Thanks to the quality of mobile phones, virtually everyone has an HD camera in their pocket nowadays. And with a cheap tripod from Amazon, you can easily film yourself.

In fact, you don't even need to buy a tripod. You can stand your phone up inside an empty roll of 2-inch masking tape if you want!

Video is perhaps the best way to engage your ICP and with a bit of effort you can quickly set yourself apart from the competition.

I would highly recommend you take the time to educate yourself on how to shoot video and how to edit it.

You don't need any fancy equipment or complicated software. You can do it all from your phone if you want. Spend 15 minutes a day for a few weeks watching YouTube videos to learn about video editing and you'll soon become more than competent.

Once you've got the basic skills you just need to follow these few simple rules and you'll start seeing results.

1. Catch their attention quickly – You have barely a second to stop potential customers from scrolling past your video, so make sure the start of the video grabs their attention.
   I recommend you don't put your logo at the start of videos, as by the time it gets to the good bit, everyone has scrolled past.
   For short videos, just dive straight into the action, then put your logo at the end.
   For longer videos, do a short catchy intro, then put your logo/title sequence, then jump into the main video. Kind of like how a James Bond film has a short action-packed scene before the opening credits with the naked shadow women.
2. Make sure the video can be understood without sound – People often watch social media videos on mute. So, add captions / subtitles if you need to.
3. Careful with the music you use – If you don't use royalty free music your video might get removed.
4. Make the video shorter – Most people (including myself) tend to make videos too long. I always try and put everything in there.

But people have very short attention spans when it comes to social media videos. So, as a rule whenever you've finished the video, take another look at it and see if you can make it shorter.
Your video is ready not when there is nothing else to add, but rather when there is nothing more to take away.
Always leave the viewer wanting more!

Case Studies

I have a love hate relationship with case studies. Part of me thinks they are often boring and old fashioned, but if I'm honest with myself, they are still hugely valuable.

Typically, a case study comes in written form, but you can do it as a video too.

If you have the time and the skills to create video case studies, then I would highly recommend it.

If you plan on just writing them up, then they can still be very powerful.

Case studies do a couple of things.

Firstly, they are great for educating potential customers on the processes involved in a successful painting and decorating project.

Secondly, they can be superb sales tools.

For example, if you are quoting for a job where you are hand painting kitchen cabinets, you could share a link to a case study from a similar job you've done before.

Doing this not only shows the customer what to expect, but it also gives them confidence that you will do a great job.

When creating a case study, I suggest you include the following information:

1. A description and photograph of what the room looked like before
2. The reason why the customer wanted to have the decorating work done and what they wanted to do with the newly transformed space
3. Any questions/concerns the customer had throughout the process and any challenges you faced
4. The reason the customer chose you to do the work
5. A photo of the finished room and a quote from the customer about how they feel now it's completed

By the way, don't fall into the trap of thinking case studies need to be long. All you need is a couple of paragraphs and you're sorted.

CONTENT CURATION

Remember how we talked about how good Farrow & Ball and Little Greene are at marketing? Well, even more good news, you can use that content to serve your ICP.

It's referred to as 'content curation'. Essentially, whenever you see an article from an interior designer, or a post about new colour trends from a paint manufacturer you should share this with your audience.

Do not pass it off as your own!

Simply share it on your social media channels and be sure to credit the source.

I love this type of content because it's really simple to do and is incredibly valuable to your ICP. It also positions you as someone who is up to date with industry trends and news. This is important to a lot of people when hiring a decorator.

USER GENERATED CONTENT (UGC)

Another type of content that is super easy to post is 'User generated content' (UGC).

Essentially, UGC is anything your customer posts about you.

So, whenever you finish a job and your customer shares pictures of their beautiful new room on their social media, make sure you share it to yours too!

If you want to take it to the next level, why not ask your customer if they can post a few pictures and a quick testimonial about what it was like to have you work there.

Your ICP will love to see what other customers think about you. So, this is one of the most powerful pieces of content you can post.

ENGAGE, ENGAGE, ENGAGE

Commenting and engaging on other people's posts is often overlooked as 'content', but trust me, it is just as important.

If you are the person / business constantly popping up with thoughtful and useful comments on different posts, then people are going to start noticing.

Let's take our ICP, Harriet, as an example.

We know Harriet is predominantly found on Facebook. We also know where she lives and what her basic interests are.

Using this information, we can work out the type of Facebook community groups she is a part of. All you need to do now is be a friendly and active member within these communities.

Doing this over a period of time will mean Harriet keeps seeing your name on her social media feed.

It will help her get to know you and trust you.

Building this relationship is key to the long-term success of your social media strategy.

Chapter 6 – Know, Like and Trust

One of the most common (and potentially overused) phrases in marketing is: *know, like and trust*.

The idea is, before someone will buy from you, they first must know, like and trust you.

This is even more crucial as a painter and decorator as most of the fears a potential customer has before hiring you could be dissolved by building up trust.

Think about it, the most common concerns anyone would have before hiring a painter and decorator are things like:

'Will they turn up on time?'

'Will they try and rip me off?'

'Can I trust them in my home?'

Building a company and brand that people know, like a trust should be a cornerstone of your social media strategy.

One of the most effective ways to do this is to post content answering the questions your customers have.

Sounds simple, doesn't it?

Well, simple as it is, not enough people do it. So, you can really separate yourself from the competition by doing this.

Schedule some time to write down every question you can think of that a customer has asked you in the past.

Write down literally everything.

The questions could be anything from, 'What can I do about the mould on my bathroom ceiling?' to, 'is it cheaper if I buy the materials?' or even, 'will you cover the furniture with dust sheets?'

Given enough time and thought, you could quite easily come up with over 100 questions with this exercise.

If you struggle thinking of all the questions you've had in the past, something I've recently started doing is to keep a Frequently Asked Questions (FAQ) log.

It's very simple to do. All you need is a little notebook or even a notes file on your phone, and whenever a customer asks you a question, write it down, and write the answer you gave too.

Sharing the questions you're asked, and the answers you give, is a great way to educate your potential customers and position yourself as a *trusted* authority in your industry.

The FAQ log is like having an unlimited source of content ideas for your social media. It's amazing!

You can answer these questions by posting photos with captions, creating videos and writing blogs / articles. You could even start a podcast if you wanted.

The point is, that if you keep popping up on your ICPs social media feed answering these questions, they are quickly going to start to *know, like and trust* you.

CHAPTER 7 – HOW TO WRITE THE PERFECT CAPTION

For thousands of years, storytelling has been the most effective way to hold people's interest and transfer information.

Social media captions are no different.

If you want to be successful on social media, you need to know how to use basic storytelling techniques.

Let's look at how to do this…

Example 1:

Image = Before and after photos of some window frames you have painted.

Standard caption = 'Some before and after pics of an exterior we've just completed. Get in touch for a free quote'

Creating a story instead:

Ask yourself, why did the customer need you? What problem did they have that needed solving?

It might be that their window frames were starting to rot, and they wanted to try and avoid having to replace them.

It could be they were jealous of the neighbour's new anthracite windows and wanted to update theirs.

Perhaps they'd just had the masonry painted and it had made their windows look a bit old and tired. So, they wanted the windows freshened up to match.

Once you've established *why* the customer needed it done, you need to explain *how* you carried out the work.

Then you create a caption that your ICP can relate to.

So, let's run the example again:

Image = Before and after photos of some window frames you have painted.

Story caption = 'Mrs Jones's windows had flaking paint and signs of rot. Rather than switching to expensive uPVC windows, Mrs Jones wanted to keep the traditional timber window frames as they were much more suited to the character of her home.

To do this, we first needed to remove all flaking paints and cut out all rotten timber.

Once we'd done this, we repaired the windows using a highly durable resin, primed and finished with 2 coats of an exterior trade paint.

Mrs Jones' window frames are now fully restored and will last for years to come.

Do your windows need some attention? Get in touch to see if we can help you too!'

See how much more powerful the story caption is?

Writing like this puts potential customers in the shoes of someone you've already worked with.

They can see exactly what problem you solve, why it needs solving, how you solve it, and what the end result will be.

Example 2:

Image = Before and after pictures of a child's bedroom

Standard caption = 'Some before and after pics of a child's bedroom we recently completed'

Enhanced caption = 'After getting great results at school my customer promised her son a bedroom makeover.

They wanted to create a more grown-up room for him, so he wasn't embarrassed to have his friends over!

We started by stripping the old wallpaper and preparing all the walls.

We then went with a dark blue on the walls AND the ceiling.

This made the room feel like a den perfect for playing video games in!'

It'll take some practice, but once you get into the habit, you'll start seeing the results. Just follow the following formula and you're well on your way.

The formula:

1. State the problem
2. Enhance the problem and explain why you're solving it
3. Explain how you solved it
4. Show the finished result and explain what difference it made to the customer

CHAPTER 8 – CUSTOMER SERVICE AND DEALING WITH BAD REVIEWS

Dealing with complaints and bad reviews that appear on your social media can be tricky.

It's all too easy to take them personally (especially when you're a sole trader)

And when you take it personally, you'll act emotionally and often make things worse.

Bad reviews are inevitable for most companies. But they can actually be great for your business.

You see, when potential customers look for reviews, they tend to skip straight past all the 5-star ones and go directly to the 1-star comments.

If a company ONLY has 5-star reviews, people don't really bother reading them. And to be honest, it looks a bit dodgy. (Too good to be true!)

So, what should you do if you get an unfavourable review or comment on your social media?

Firstly, take a breath and separate yourself from the comment.

Try to look at it as a business problem that needs a logical solution.

Now you need to respond to the comment / review.

At this stage you need to apologise that they are unhappy and find out how you can help resolve this issue.

Try to take the conversation away from social media if you can, as sometimes the person with the issue will act up even more because they know they have an audience.

The key now is to listen to their complaint and then ask them the following question:

'How can I resolve this problem for you?'

Now they are in a position where they need to tell YOU exactly what they want and work out how you should do it.

Once you have this information, you then need to make a commercial decision.

Is it worth you doing it or not?

This is a decision you need to make logically. Not emotionally.

So, take your time!

Things you must NOT do…

1. Argue with them. Trying to win an argument with an unhappy customer never ends well. Even if you know you're 100% right, then you still shouldn't argue. Potential customers looking at the reviews don't want to deal with an argumentative tradesperson.
2. Try to make them change / remove the review. The more you ask, the more they will dig their heels in. So don't do it!

3. Ignore it. If you haven't responded to the complaints, it looks like you don't care and that you just run off with people's money.

What should you do after you've resolved the issue?

Once the customer is happy, it is fair to ask them if they wouldn't mind updating their review stating that you have resolved their problem. 9 times out of 10 they will do this without being prompted.

It is likely they won't change the review from 1 star to 5 stars, but that's not what you want.

What you want is the chain of messages showing publicly that you received a poor review, and you then responded quickly and professionally to resolve the issue. And that the customer then upgraded their review to 3 or 4 stars.

It's interactions like this that people read before hiring someone.

Everybody knows that no business is perfect.

Problems are inevitable, it's how you deal with them that separates good businesses from great ones.

Chapter 9 – How often should you post?

How often should you post on social media?

Type this question into Google and you get over 3 BILLION results!

The answers tend to range from 1-2 times a week up to 5-10 times a day.

I don't think putting a number on it is helpful.

You shouldn't force yourself to post a certain number of times every day or week.

If you've got nothing worth posting, then don't post anything.

You can tell when a company is forcing content out, and it's not a good look. (Trust me, I've been there!)

They'll post rubbish like:

'It's national squirrel appreciation day! Here's Dave from the office looking out the window trying to see one. Have you ever seen a squirrel?'

So, what is worth posting?

Think about it from the perspective of your audience? What do they want to see on their social media feed?

As we've said before, they want to see things that are informative, entertaining or help them connect to people. It's called 'social' media after all.

Whenever you have something that fits any of these categories, post it.

If that's once a week. Great.

If that's 5 times a day. Great.

PS: Ridiculous as it sounds, national squirrel appreciation day is a real thing. It's celebrated in the USA on January 21st.

CHAPTER 10 – HOW TO RUN A SUCCESSFUL COMPETITION

One of the most effective ways to give your social media a boost is to run a competition.

To make sure your business sees the maximum benefit from running a competition, there are a few important things you need to do.

Set Your Objective

When launching a competition, you need to be clear on your objective. This means you need to decide what you want to get out of it.

Common objectives include: Increase exposure, gain followers or collecting email addresses.

Deciding your objective helps us with the next tip.

Keep It Simple!

Entering a competition should be quick and easy.

All too often I see competition posts where you have to do all sorts to enter.

You've seen the type. They usually look something like this…

'To enter: like, share, tag 3 friends, comment with your favourite gif and follow these 4 accounts'

Don't do this.

When you try and get too much out of a competition people won't enter.

Choose your objective and then set the entering process accordingly.

For example:

Increase exposure = like and share to enter

Gain followers = Follow and share to enter. Or follow and tag a friend to enter.

Collect email addresses = Click this link and enter your email.

PICK YOUR PLATFORM

Competitions tend to work best when you run them on just 1 platform.

So, choose the platform according to your objective.

If you want to maximise exposure, Twitter is great because of the retweet function.

If you want people to click a link and give you their email address then don't use Instagram, because you can't post links on Instagram.

If you want to focus on local people, then Facebook is good because you can post the competition in local groups.

If you want to gain new followers, Instagram works well because you can ask people to tag their friends in the comments.

Also, don't forget to take into consideration what platform your ICP uses. If Instagram is great for your ICP, then make sure you use Insta for your competition.

By the way, there is nothing wrong with using other platforms to advertise the fact you're running a competition elsewhere.

For example, say you are running a competition on Facebook, and you have loads of followers on Twitter. You could post on your Twitter saying you're running a competition on your Facebook page and give them a link to find it. This can help you quickly move some of your following from one platform to another.

This is very useful when new platforms come along, and you want to build up your audience.

PICK A PRIZE THAT APPEALS TO YOUR IDEAL CUSTOMER

One of the most common mistakes I see when people run a competition is offering a prize that attracts the wrong sort of person.

If you're a decorator, don't give away prizes like tins of paint, brushes or Brewers vouchers.

This sort of prize will attract DIYers and other decorators. Both are not much good for your business.

Think about what your ICP would like.

Perhaps you could offer to wallpaper a feature wall for free, or a voucher for a local interiors store.

Prize bundles always work well as the perceived value is high.

In terms of budget, I find that £25 - £50 is a sweet spot. Anything less and it isn't that appealing. Anything more and you don't get enough entries to warrant the extra money spent.

NB: If you are offering to complete some work as the prize then you ideally want to be able to do it in half a day.

SET A TIME FRAME

Personally, I find most success running competitions for 7 days. It gives enough time for most people to see it, but it's not so long that people forget about it. Plus, I find that entries after 7 days are very few and far between. So, it's not really worth it.

When you run a 7-day competition I suggest you do the initial launch post, followed by reminder posts at the halfway point, at 48 hours before the end, 24 hours and 1 hour before it closes.

Flash competitions that run for 24 or 48 hours are popular, but if you do this, you'll find a lot of people are disappointed they didn't see the post in time. Plus, you significantly reduce the number of entries you get.

Remember your Terms and conditions

Don't forget to cover yourself with some basic T&Cs. If you are offering to do some work for the winner then be sure to set a maximum travel distance for the work, set an expiry date for doing it (1 year is fine) and be clear on whether they need to supply the materials.

If it is a prize that you'll need to post, then consider making it only eligible for UK residents (or wherever you live).

And of course, be very clear on when the deadline for entries is, and when you'll draw the winner.

Bonus tip: Kingsumo

There is a great free app that you can use to run competitions called King sumo. Link below.

Here you can set up your competition and people must enter their email address to take part.

Kingsumo gives you a link to a private page where people can enter the competition. You can then share this link across all your social media platforms.

This is the best way to run a competition across multiple platforms.

At the end of the competition, you'll have a list of GDPR compliant email addresses.

After you've drawn the winner, it's a good idea to send 1 email to all the other people who entered. Use this email to thank them for entering and give them a consolation prize. Something like a code for 10% off future decorating work would be ideal. As you want it to lead to some work!

https://kingsumo.com/

CHAPTER 11 – PUBLIC RELATIONS (PR)

One day, someone asks on a social media forum for recommendations on a plasterer.

To help, you recommend someone you've worked with.

You didn't know it at the time, but your ICP saw this small act of kindness.

3 months later that same ICP was hiring you to do some work...one of the contributing factors to you getting the job is that she'd seen you regularly in forums helping out where you can.

Of course, one good deed was not the only thing that made her choose you.

But simple things like this shape how people perceive you and your business.

So, how does PR fit into this?

PR stands for 'Public Relations'.

PR is the message you and your business put out into the world.

And it controls how everyone perceives you. Including your ICP!

For example:

If somebody posted about how you did some free decorating for a charity project, that would be good PR.

If a video popped up on YouTube of you sleeping on the job, that would be bad PR.

Of course, these are the extreme ends of the scale.

You're not going to do charity work every weekend…and you're unlikely to sleeping on the job!

Anyway, think of PR as a scale that you're constantly moving on.

Help someone in a forum…add 1 point

Argue with someone about something pointless on Twitter. Lose 2 points.

Post about how you've sponsored the local children's football team, add 5 points.

…and so on.

Building up good PR takes time and consistency.

You won't realise it straight away...and sometimes it might not come back for years.

In fact, most of what you do may seem invisible.

But it's this 'invisible PR' that can help you build a stronger company and brand.

CHAPTER 12 – MANAGING YOUR BRAND

In the previous chapter we touched on how good PR can support your brand.

But PR is not *all* of your brand.

Whenever I need to explain brand, I explain it like this:

Have you ever walked into an unfamiliar shop and before you even see the prices on anything you think to yourself…'I bet it's expensive in here'

Or have you ever looked at a website that is just one page, has low quality images and thought, 'well, this is either a scam, a company that hasn't traded in a long time or whatever they sell must be cheap and nasty'

This is 'brand'.

So, as a company owner, how do you build the brand you want?

The first thing to do when building a brand is to decide on your personal values and build your brand on that.

You have to be honest with yourself. If your brand doesn't match your personal values, you will be in a constant wrestling match with yourself and always pretending to be something you're not.

This simply won't work.

NB: If you are an employee of a larger company, you will find you are much happier working for a company that shares the same values as you do.

For example, if attention to detail is very important to you, but the company you work for values speed of work over precision of work, then you'll likely be unhappy working there.

The second thing to know about brand is:

Everything you put out to the world, is a reflection/indicator of your brand and values.

This is amplified on social media.

ESTABLISHING YOUR VALUES

Let's say you are a self-employed painter & decorator, and you establish your key personal values are as follows:

Honesty and integrity

Cleanliness

Attention to detail

Not settling for anything less than perfect

As a decorator, these would be pretty solid values to have, and they are well suited to the occupation.

A MUDDLED MESSAGE

So, let's say you've established your true values and you are building your brand accordingly. You specialise in high end work that demands the utmost attention to detail and going above and beyond for the customer. You are expensive, but you are worth it.

But hang on a minute, you seem to keep losing jobs to cheap painters who value speed over quality.

And why do you keep getting messages on Facebook asking if you can paint a whole house next Tuesday for £200 cash?

What's going on?

Well, this is the part where a lot of people trip up.

The actual work they produce is perfectly in line with their values and deserves the expensive price tag. However, how they present themselves on social media is not.

As a decorator, you may never rip off a customer, always be clean and tidy, always strive for the perfect finish and never miss a detail.

But if your social media includes videos of rental bashing jobs, your photos are blurry and every picture of you shows you wearing t-shirts covered in 6 months' worth of paint, then your brand is muddled.

You're showing the world you are not fussed on details like good quality photography and clean branded t-shirts, you're showing you're happy to do the odd quick job, even though you claim to always take your time and do things to perfection.

Your product/service is brilliant. But you're presenting it in the wrong way and to the wrong ICP.

You're trying to sell a £5,000 designer handbag in Primark.

The handbag might be the most beautiful bag ever created, but if you stick it in the clearance aisle in Primark two things will happen.

1. People will be shocked by the price because everything else about the place indicates it is a cheap/value store.
2. Nobody will buy it because they are the wrong target market

Everything you do on social media affects your brand and therefore your true values

It is crucial to remember this applies to everything, not just the actual decorating work.

A good question to ask yourself whenever you're going to post on social media is:

Is this in line with my values?

For example:

Does the quality of this photo match the quality of the work I deliver? Have I spent time editing it and making sure there is no rubbish in the background?

Does this video look professional? Has it got my company branding on it? Are the edits all clean?

Once you start asking yourself questions like this, you'll start building a brand that truly matches your values and your work.

This will then lead to more of the customers you want and fewer time wasters!

Plus, as a bonus every business decision suddenly becomes a lot easier. As when everything is based on your core values you won't want to compromise them!

CHAPTER 13 – SHOULD YOU USE SCHEDULING TOOLS?

Now you're creating all this incredible content and you've got your brand nailed you might be considering using a scheduling tool to strategically post it to each social media network.

If you've not heard of this sort of thing, they are quite simple.

Essentially, you use a third-party piece of software to create your social media posts, and then schedule the date and time for when those pieces of content should be posted on to each social media network.

As with everything like this, there are pros and cons.

First, let's talk about price.

Scheduling tools range from being free, for very basic versions, up to thousands of pounds for more complex versions that can handle multiple accounts and users.

If you're a sole trader, the basic free version may well be enough for what you need, so they are well worth a go.

If you're a larger company and want multiple people to use it, then you'll need to do some research and find the best fit for you.

Now we've got price out of the way. Let's go back to the original chapter question then: Should you use scheduling tools?

Personally, I like them. I've used a few different ones for my own work and for the companies I've worked for, and they are all reasonably intuitive.

The biggest benefits in my opinion are that you can schedule to post at the times your ICP is more likely to be online (particularly useful if your ICP is online late in the evening and you're trying to relax and not look at your phone) and it takes some of the stress away from thinking you have to create and post content all the time.

If you set aside a couple of hours, you'll be able to schedule all your social media posts for an entire month if you want.

This gives you the peace of mind that no matter how busy you are, you still have your social media strategy running in the background.

However, if you are going to take this approach, you need to be careful not to fall into the mindset of creating content for content's sake. If you find yourself looking up when National Squirrel appreciation day is, then you know you're in trouble.

Remember your content always needs to serve your ICP and what they want.

If you are going to use a scheduling tool, then I suggest you mix in a healthy number of 'unscheduled' posts.

A good way to do it would be to schedule in the content where you are answering your FAQs and maybe some photos/videos/articles that could inspire some design ideas for your ICP. This sort of thing could be the backbone of your content.

On top of that you should then sprinkle in posts showing what you're doing on a daily basis. Behind the scenes videos are always interesting. Before and after photos of jobs are always great to see as soon as they've been completed.

Finally, please don't forget that just because you scheduled the post 2 weeks ago, it doesn't mean you don't have to respond to the comments.

If someone has taken the time to comment on your post, you should always try to respond. Even if it's just to say thank you.

You don't have to respond to the comments straight away. Afterall, you're using a scheduling tool so you don't need to be on social media at that particular time. But you should be aiming to respond within 24 hours.

Chapter 14 – Paid Advertising

This book is written to be evergreen. So, I'm not going to tell you the step-by-step process for setting up paid adverts (ads) on each platform.

Who knows, by the time you read this, Facebook, Instagram and Twitter might not even exist!

Just know that social media platforms make their profit with these ads. This means there are teams of people who have the sole purpose of making it as easy as possible for people like you to spend money on paid ads.

In fact, it's sometimes too easy to set them up. Often, you'll be presented with a single button to 'promote' or 'boost' your post.

This leads me neatly on to what I am going to talk about in this chapter.

You should never just click a button and turn a post into an ad.

Good advertising takes planning.

Whether you're creating an ad for TV, a newspaper, radio, billboard or anything else it is the same.

And that includes social media ads!

IDENTIFY YOUR TARGET

As usual, the first thing to do is to identify your target. Fortunately for us, we've got Harriet (and you have your own ICP).

Social media offers incredible targeting functions. And they are only getting better.

This means you can be really specific about who you want to see your ads. And you should be REALLY SPECIFIC!

Use everything you know about your ICP to target exactly the right potential customers.

For example, if we take 3 very basic factors: age, gender and location we would set the following parameters to target Harriet:

Age: 65-75

Gender: Female

Location: Oxford

Now, when you start putting this information in, there will be a voice in your head saying 'but I don't want to lose potential work from men, or younger people'

You need to disregard that voice because it'll waste your money.

To get the best deal from ads you want only the right people seeing and clicking on your post.

Example:

If I spent £10 advertising to women like Harriet who are 65-75 and live in Oxford, then the advert might reach 10,000 who fit that profile. From which, 50 of them might click on the advert.

However, if I spent that same £10 and added men into the equation, then I might reach 5,000 men and 5,000 women.

And because men aren't my ICP, they won't click as much. I might end up with just 10 clicks from males. And to make things worse, because only half as many women saw the ad, I'll only get 25 clicks from females.

Giving me a total of 35 clicks. 15 fewer than when I was specific on my target ICP.

To summarise, be specific on your target or you'll just end up wasting money.

SET YOUR OBJECTIVE...AND STICK TO IT!

Is the goal of your ad a short term fix? Such as getting a quick boost in enquiries?

Or are you doing something to help your long-term strategy?

You shouldn't do both in one ad, so this is the first decision you need to make.

If you want a boost in enquiries then your advert should be short, concise and simply trying to get them to click and take that action.

You shouldn't be trying to sell them on the ins and outs of your services with the ad itself. You'll do the selling when they land on your website or start messaging you.

NB: If you are directing people to your website, make sure when they get there, they have a clear idea of what to do next. Don't just send them to your homepage.

It is a good idea to build a specific page for them to land on that continues from the advert. This page should quickly tell them all the reasons why they should choose you and give them a clear and simple way to get in contact.

If your objective is part of your long-term strategy, for example, you want to build trust and authority, then your ad can include more detail and doesn't necessarily need to tell your ICP to take any action right now.

A good example of these two approaches can be seen in TV adverts from big companies like banks.

Sometimes you'll see an ad for a bank like Lloyds that offers £100 if you switch your current account to them.

This is an example of a short-term objective. They are simply looking to boost their numbers a bit.

At other times you'll see an advert from Lloyds that seemingly makes no sense. It's just a black horse running along a beach or something. It might talk about some of the charity work they do or explain how they are adding more staff to their branches, but it doesn't directly ask you to take any action. It doesn't say, 'Open an account today'

Ultimately, a healthy mix of ads with short-term and long-term goals are a good idea.

DECIDE ON THE PHOTO/VIDEO AND TEXT BEFORE YOU START SETTING UP THE AD

Do your first few drafts in a word document on your laptop or in a notes file on your phone. Don't just open up the app and start winging it!

Consider multiple pictures/videos for the ad. Write out a few potential pieces of text to use. Refine and edit it over a couple of days. Think about what would appeal to your ICP and consider if the ad fits the rest of your strategy and brand.

Most importantly, don't rush it!

A well prepared advert can easily outperform a bad one by 10x.

This is the difference between getting 20 enquiries from a £20 advert or 200 enquiries. It could mean thousands of pounds of extra revenue for your business. So, take the time to do it well.

Nail the Headline

Establish a few keywords you want to use in your headline, then try and think of at least 10 possible headlines.

Once you have at least 10 options, then decide on your best one.

NB: It is not uncommon for advertisers (including me) to write out 50-100 potential headlines for an advert. Often, you'll find the best ones come to you after you've exhausted all the obvious ones.

A good headline can easily increase your enquiries by 5x on its own.

Give it the time and respect it deserves.

Run the Ad for at Least a Week

It will take the algorithm a few days to work out exactly how to get the most people clicking on your advert. I would typically suggest you run a 7-day campaign spending as little as possible per day to start. If you find the advert is giving you good results you can choose to increase your spend or extend the length of the campaign. If not, you can try something else and you haven't lost much money.

DON'T GIVE UP

Finally, remember not to get disheartened if your ad doesn't do as well as you'd hoped. Advertising is tricky and takes a lot of trial and error.

Most adverts fail. Not just for decorators. For everyone. Including me.

You certainly shouldn't expect much success from your first few adverts. Be patient and stick with it. You will get there!

The key is to keep testing and improving until you find something that works.

Fail often but fail cheaply.

Then when you find the advert that works, you double down on it and make some serious money.

PS: If you ever want me to review your ads and give you some ideas for improving them, feel free to send them over. jon@jmears.co.uk

Chapter 15 – Measuring your Return On Investment (ROI)

There is a simple formula to measure your return on investment (ROI):

ROI % = (Profit made – money spent on ads) ÷ money spent on ads x 100

I'll give you an example, if you spend £20 on social media ads which gives you 5 enquiries. And from those you get 2 jobs with a total profit of £500, your formula looks like the following:

(£500 profit - £20 spent on ads) ÷ £20 spent on ads x 100 = 2,400% ROI

If, however, you got the same results, but paid £480 on ads, your formula would look like this:

(£500 profit - £480 spent on ads) ÷ £480 spent on ads x 100 = 4.16% ROI.

If you don't like doing the maths, don't worry. Search ROI calculator on Google and there are plenty of websites that'll do the calculation for you. All you have to do is enter the amount you spent and the profit you made.

Whilst the formula might be simple, getting the information you need (money spent and profit made) can be a little trickier.

You see, social media marketing is more than just paid ads. And typically, the reason a customer hires you is down to a combination of factors, not just because they saw 1 ad.

With this in mind, how can you even begin to measure the ROI on your social media marketing efforts?

The first thing you need to do is start keeping track of how each customer heard about you and what made them get in touch.

Be aware it's rarely a cut and dry thing. Even if the customer says you were recommended by a friend, there will have been other contributing factors as to why they got in touch with you.

After they received the recommendation, they likely had a look at your website and your social media.

They then might have put off calling you for a couple of weeks, but during that time they might have seen your posts on social media. They could even have seen one of your social media ads!

All these things came together to ultimately get you an enquiry, so, at first glance you might put it down as 'word of mouth' but with a bit of digging you could find out your social media and website helped.

Of course, the reverse of this could also happen. A customer might have received a recommendation for you and forgot to follow up on it. Then a week later your ad popped up on social media and they hit the 'enquire now' button, which makes you think they were a direct result of the ad.

For the sake of simplicity, I suggest you put your social media marketing spend in with all the rest of the spending you do for marketing. Whether that's leaflets, website maintenance, van signwriting, business cards etc.

Then all you want to do is try and make the ROI % go up each month.

It doesn't matter where you start, just focus on improving the number.

Example:

Let's say in January you spend £200 on marketing and secure 5 jobs with a total profit of £3,000.

(£3,000 profit - £200 spent on ads) ÷ £200 spent on marketing x 100 = 1,400% ROI.

Then in February you spend £75 and secure 2 jobs making £1,200 profit.

(£1,200 profit - £75 spent on ads) ÷ £75 spent on marketing x 100 = 1,500% ROI.

You see, even though in February you spent less money on marketing and made less profit, your ROI % was actually higher. Having this information means that you know that the marketing work you did in February was actually more effective than what you did in January.

Armed with this information you can be smarter with your money in March!

CHAPTER 16 – COMMON MISTAKES YOU NEED TO AVOID

When you download a social media app for the first time you don't get tutorial videos on how to act on there. You just have to work it out for yourself.

In fairness, it should be simple.

It's called social media. Emphasis on the 'social'.

As a general rule, I think it helps to treat social media like any other social event.

Before you do something on social media, ask yourself if you'd act like that at a party or down the pub with your mates. If the answer is no, then don't do whatever you were going to do.

Here are a few things I see regularly on social media that you should avoid doing:

PRETENDING TO BE SOMETHING YOU'RE NOT

If you want people to *know, like and trust* you, then you need to be authentic.

If you're funny, be funny.

If you're a bit of a geek, be a bit of a geek.

Too many people try to copy others and act differently on social media.

If you're a 50-year-old decorator called Steve and you're recording yourself talking to camera, don't feel like you have to act like those high energy 14 year old YouTubers.

People trust authenticity. And if you're putting on an act then people will see right through it.

99% of decorators I've ever spoken to have told me the reason they get so many referrals and repeat custom is because of their personality.

I'd wager that you're the same.

You're good at building rapport with customers in real life, so all you need to do is continue being yourself on social media and you're sorted.

NOT RESPONDING TO COMMENTS

If somebody has taken the time to comment on your post, or has sent you a direct message, it's common courtesy to respond.

If someone said something to you in a real-life situation you wouldn't just ignore them, so don't do it on social media.

If you don't know what to say, just put 'thank you for your comment'

Bragging

Yes, I'm sure you're a brilliant decorator but nobody likes a show-off. Of course, if you've achieved something you're proud of then absolutely put in on social media. But make sure it's not all you post. And don't be a 'topper'. A topper is someone who has done everything you've done before, just slightly better. You know what I mean. If you've swam the channel, they've drank it.

Don't bad mouth other decorators

Talking ill of other decorators (especially your local competition) just looks bad on you.

Nobody wants to hire someone who posts nasty messages about other people in their trade.

Oh, and nobody cares if you do or don't use tape. So don't be that boring bloke constantly going on about it in the forums.

Don't be 'Mr Right'

I'm sure you're very clever and incredibly funny. But you don't have to prove it at every opportunity. Don't take the mick out of people for not knowing something that you think is 'simple' or 'basic'. Don't pick people up on bad grammar. It's just not that important. Don't try to put a stupid 'funny' comment on every post. And don't argue your opinion to the death every time someone challenges you. Even if you are right, you can still look like a muppet.

Stop attracting other decorators

Being part of a community of decorators is great. You can learn new techniques and help fellow brothers and sisters of the brush. But please don't forget that other decorators are not who you are trying to attract to your business, so you shouldn't be hounding them to like your Facebook page.

Always remember your content needs to be geared towards your ICP.

Don't complain about customers

Even if you have a separate profile and you don't mention any names, you still shouldn't moan about customers or your job in general. These things have a tendency to come out over time and the results are never good.

We all need to vent from time to time and that's ok. Just don't do it on social media!

CONCLUSION

Throughout this book I've talked a lot about very serious sounding things like strategies, brand management and ICPs.

I want to finish by telling you to remember that it's only social media.

There are bigger and more important things in the world, so don't panic if you think your social media hasn't been very good so far. And don't stress if you post something you perhaps shouldn't have.

Not everything you do on social media is going to be perfect. And it doesn't need to be.

You're not a world leader. You're not going to be scrutinized for every little thing you do.

So put yourself out there. Have fun and try new things. If it doesn't work, then fine. No harm done.

As long as you commit to keep learning and improving then you'll be amazed how far you can go.

My final piece of advice is this:

Social media is a long game.

Building your social media is like building your company. It takes time and patience.

Little and often is the key. If you spend just 15 minutes a day working on your social media, your business will be in a very different place in a year. And it'll be almost unrecognisable in 5.

About The Author

This is the part of the book where for some reason people start talking about themselves in the third person. (I'm not going to do that)

Who am I?

I started in sales in 2006. Since then, I've had a number of sales and marketing roles across several companies. Some of which I was very successful. Some not so much!

I began writing in 2020 primarily to help professional painters & decorators with their sales and marketing. Something that for some reason is not part of the college courses!

My other objective is to help raise the profile of the industry that I love (Painting & Decorating) and help tradesmen across the world get the recognition they deserve.

So why listen to what I have to say?

Well, since I started in sales, I have consumed 1,000's of hours of content on the subject. I've read hundreds of books, listened to countless podcasts and been on more boring sales courses than I can remember.

Most importantly, it's been my full-time job for over 10 years. Which means I've made a hell of a lot of mistakes. All of which I have learned from and used to improve.

Even if you are a more successful salesperson than me, it doesn't mean I can't help you. After all, even Tiger Woods has a coach.

More info

For more information on me and loads of free sales and marketing tips, check out my website (and sign up to my mailing list!): www.jmears.co.uk/ebook

To see my other books, (Including 'Sales & Marketing for Decorators', 'Advertising for Decorators' and 'The 28 day marketing plan for decorators') have a look at my Amazon author page: https://www.amazon.co.uk/Mr-Jon-Mears/e/B08LHDN1DD?ref_=dbs_p_ebk_r00_abau_000000

GET IN TOUCH

Email: jonmearsblogs@gmail.com

Twitter: @JonMears10

Instagram: @jmears.co.uk

Facebook: facebook.com/jmears.co.uk

Facebook group: Search – 'Sales & Marketing support for painters and decorators'

YouTube Channel name: 'Sales & Marketing for Decorators'

LinkedIn: linkedin.com/in/jon-mears/

www.ingramcontent.com/pod-product-compliance
Lightning Source LLC
LaVergne TN
LVHW050602160826
845677LV00011B/2420